A window on WALTON-on-Thames

J. L. & D. M. BARKER

Introduction

The name Walton is thought to mean "town of the Britons", suggesting a pre-Saxon settlement here. Until 1851, the parish was a very large one of almost 7,000 acres, but sparsely populated by a largely agricultural community. The village of Walton consisted of Church Street and Bridge Street, with a few shops at the north end of High Street on the east side, the Ashley Park estate occupying all the land on the west side of the street. The area was somewhat isolated by the lack of good roads – a situation partially alleviated in 1750 by the construction of the first Walton Bridge. The coming of the railway in 1838 did much to stimulate the village's development, while the 20th century has seen pronounced changes in the character and layout of the town – notably the development of two new major streets in 1933 and 1965.

It is appropriate that this book should appear in the year in which we celebrate the centenary of the British picture postcard, as many of the illustrations have been taken from postcards produced by some of the excellent local photographers to whom Walton historians are greatly indebted. In view of Walton's major contribution to the early film industry, next year's centenary of the cinematograph must also not be forgotten.

For those interested in Walton's past, three excellent earlier books are still available: "Victorian and Edwardian Camera Studies" by Morag Barton; the Walton and Weybridge Local History Society's publication, "A Short History of Walton-on-Thames" by Michael Blackman; and "A Dictionary of Local History" by George Greenwood.

Both the Local History Society and Elmbridge Museum have been of invaluable assistance during the preparation of this work, and I have drawn extensively on the memories of local people, past and present – notably the reminiscences of the late Gladys Ward and Frank Andrews, preserved in the museum's files. We have also been fortunate again in the generosity of one of the country's foremost postcard dealers and of several major local collectors.

As in our earlier books, I have tried to follow a topographical arrangement here, which I hope will prove easy for the reader to follow.

JOCELYN BARKER
November 1994

FRONT COVER
Centre: The drinking fountain, Church Street - the gift of Richard Wilcox Boyle of Portland House, Hersham Road, erected January 1899. Photograph c.1910.
Left: Walton Bridge c.1905; Bridge Street looking west c.1902; The Swan Hotel, Manor Road, c.1910.
Right: The Anglers and wharf c.1905; High Street looking north c.1905; Ingram's Corner, The Halfway, c.1905.

"THE FISHING SPOT" c.1910
The punt is moored in a favourite location for local fishermen. Beyond it is the third Walton Bridge, built in 1864, and on the left the small footbridge carrying the towpath over the entrance to The Backwater (now Walton Marina) and Rosewell's Boathouse, now occupied by Rosewell Computers Ltd. An advertisement of c.1900-1910 claims that it was "Patronised by the present Emperor and Empress of Russia, and H.S.H. Prince Louis of Battenberg". (The future Czar and Czarina stayed with Prince Louis at Elm Grove in 1894.) The advertisement boasts a "New and Commodious Boat House, close to Walton Bridge, containing Ladies' and Gents' Dressing Rooms and Private Lockers. Established 1850." Although John Rosewell is listed in directories of the 1860s as a fisherman there is in fact no mention of boat-building at this period, and this business was apparently established by his eldest son Sedgwick Rosewell about 1885.

THE RIVER THAMES, JANUARY 1925
The view from the Shepperton bank of the Thames near Walton Bridge across the river towards the water works off Walton Lane conflicts with the official statement of the Thames Conservancy at the time that there was no flooding. On Friday, 2nd January, 1925, the "Surrey Herald" reported that "On Monday...the river was a mile wide...", while by Tuesday, "All around Walton Bridge is water, the historic Cowey having entirely disappeared, and from the high ground at Oatlands to the Water Co's embankment now appears to be the width of the river. " Whiffen & Co., the Shepperton estate agents, probably had few takers for their proffered "Plots to Let...for Bungalows" over the New Year period!

THE WHARF, 1904

This photograph by Walter F.J. Hodgson of Kingston-on-Thames was used on a Christmas card in 1904. The wharf is now used only for pleasure boats, but in the early part of the 20th century Thames barges similar to the one illustrated loaded and unloaded here. One of the largest users was the Walton-on-Thames & Weybridge Gas Company, whose coal supplies were unloaded here, originally by hand but later using a steam-driven crane. The public drawdock was reserved for watering livestock, and boats were left here at the owners' risk. Beyond The Swan and The Anglers can be seen Rosewell's lower boathouse, to which a second storey was added at some time between 1904 and 1908.

WALTON TOWN REGATTA, 10th AUGUST, 1910

The "Walton Mile" provides the only straight mile on the Thames other than Henley, and is still the scene of the Amateur Regatta first held in 1862. In 1910 the "Surrey Herald" reported that "Glorious weather and a long interesting programme resulted in this year's Town Regatta...proving one of the most enjoyable riverside festivals that Walton has seen for a number of years." The first Town Regatta took place c.1887. Held in late August, it was open to local watermen and others not eligible for the Amateur Regatta, and included many "novelty" events such as the canoe steeplechase, the costume race and climbing the greasy pole. The day ended with a firework display in the evening. Local people are shown here gathering near the finishing line. Around 1900, skiffs and punts like those seen here could be hired from three boathouses and one mooring place in Walton at 1s (5p) for the first hour and 6d (2½p) for each subsequent hour. The event lapsed during the First World War and efforts to revive it afterwards were unsuccessful.

NORTH-WEST WALTON-ON-THAMES c.1925

An aerial view by Surrey Flying Services of Croydon shows this area before the development of New Zealand Avenue and Hepworth Way. Mount Felix was still standing, but the Ridgeway and Rivermount developments had recently been built in the grounds of the mansion. To the right of the centre of the picture are the famous Hepworth Film Studios in Hurst Grove, in the area now occupied by the Centre. Towards the top of the picture is a gas holder. The new Walton and Weybridge Gas Company established its works here in 1869, with access from the end of the present Annett Road. In 1887 the site was extended by the purchase of properties in Chapel Street (now Manor Road). This included the old Methodist chapel built in 1845, and a new entrance was constructed on the site of the chapel, but the associated schoolrooms were used by the Gas Company as stores. When the gas industry was nationalised in 1949 the production plant here was dismantled, but the gas holders and stores mentioned above **survived until the early 1970s.**

ENTRANCE TO MOUNT FELIX c.1913

Shortly before the First World War, a photographer from Ashford recorded this view from Oatlands Drive, showing its junction with Bridge Street. The lodges in the foreground had once marked the entrance to the carriage drive of Oatlands Park. Until 1846, when this became a public road, local residents had to use a lane further to the east. The original entrance to Mount Felix opened onto Bridge Street near the end of this lane, but about 1869 Ann Ingram, then owner of Mount Felix, purchased land at the junction of Oatlands Drive, including one of the lodges, for the purpose of constructing the entrance shown here. The gate pillars bore the Ingram family arms and were surmounted by wrought iron lanterns. These lanterns and the elaborate iron gates were sold and taken to the U.S.A. in the 1920s when the estate was developed for housing, but the pillars survive in their original position.

MOUNT FELIX c.1920

Seen here from the rear in a photograph by Edmund Jordan of Bridge Street, the mansion later known as Mount Felix originated in a house built by Harry Rodney (father of Admiral Lord Rodney) c.1715. This house was reconstructed in the Italian style by the 5th Earl of Tankerville in 1837-40. At the foot of the tower was a "porte cochére" - a porch through which a coach could be driven, enabling passengers to be picked up or dropped off under cover. The architect was Charles Barry and the cost approximately £80,000. The Earl gave his remodelled mansion the name "Mount Felix", by which it is still remembered. John Mason Cook, son of the founder of the well-known travel agency, bought the house in 1898 and installed the first telephone in Walton, but died in 1899. In 1905 a scheme for the local Council to purchase the house for use as Council Offices was frustrated by the opposition of the ratepayers. After the declaration of war in August 1914 it was requisitioned by the War Department, and initially used to house British troops until May 1915.

A WARD AT MOUNT FELIX, CHRISTMAS 1917

The New Zealand War Contingent Association took over Mount Felix in June 1915 and converted it for use as a military hospital, which opened at the end of July. In September 1915, responsibility passed to the Army Medical Services and Mount Felix became officially the New Zealand No. 2 General Hospital. Although run by the New Zealand military authorities, the hospital was partly staffed by Voluntary Aid Detachments (V.A.D.s). The photograph shows the 1917 Christmas festivities in one of the huts built to extend the accommodation available. The hospital closed in March 1920.

HOSPITAL FOOTBRIDGE c.1917

In January 1916, five timber and asbestos huts were erected on the land south of Bridge Street, between Oatlands Drive and the River Thames, to serve as additional wards for the hospital at Mount Felix. These wards each accommodated about 40 patients, and a footbridge and covered walkway were constructed to link them with the main buildings north of Bridge Street. A new cook-house was also established in the hutted area. The footbridge is shown here from the approach to Walton Bridge, with the junction of Oatlands Drive beyond it. In the left foreground is one of the iron "City posts" or "coal tax posts" erected following an Act of 1861 to mark the boundary of the Metropolitan Police District. Until 1889, duty was payable on coal and wine passing into this area. The post can still be seen in its original position at the Walton end of the bridge.

NEW ZEALAND AVENUE c.1935

In 1923, Walton U.D.C. conceived plans for a bypass across the Ashley Park estate from Walton Bridge to the south end of the High Street. The purchase of the land was agreed in 1926, but the necessary funds and M.o.T. approval were not available for road construction. In August 1931 the estimated cost, exclusive of soil sewer, was £13,627. The road was to be called New Zealand Avenue. Work commenced in 1933 and the official opening took place on 9th November, 1935. On the left of the picture is the garage first opened in the 1920s by R.W.H. Marris Ltd. in a former scene-painting and construction shop of the recently-closed Hepworth Studios. It changed hands in 1933 and again in 1935/36, when it became Bridge Motors and a new forecourt and pumps were installed at this end of the building. Vickers used the building for making parts for Wellington bombers during the Second World War, after which it was re-opened as a garage by John Heath, who ran a small garage at The Halfway. Its new name, Hersham and Walton Motors, was shortened to H.W.M., and this name became well known in motor-racing circles. Active involvement with racing ceased after John Heath's death in 1956, but the company still specialises in high-performance cars.

WALTON & WEYBRIDGE COUNCIL OFFICES 1966

In 1938 the Walton and Weybridge Urban District Council had purchased a plot of land on New Zealand Avenue for £13,250, for the erection of a public hall and fire station, but the outbreak of war the following year naturally resulted in the postponement of this project. The Council decided in 1954 to set aside four acres of the site for new offices, but the plans were not finally approved until 1962. The building, with its three symmetrical wings, was completed in 1966 at a final cost of £286,758, and opened by Princess Margaret on 19th October. Superseded in 1992 by the new Civic Offices in Esher, it was demolished in 1993 and Sainsbury's Homebase built on the site.

NEW ZEALAND AVENUE c.1955

In 1939 the New Zealand Government sent Walton a gift of trees to be planted along New Zealand Avenue. These would have made the road more of an avenue in the true sense, but they were found to be unsuitable and were planted instead in Stompond Lane Garden. In the foreground is the Regal cinema, built in 1937 by Mr. Morris to the design of the celebrated cinema architect Mr. C. Edmund Wilford. The building was intended "to typify the charming rural surroundings of Walton by the blending of a modern and Georgian treatment", while the facade incorporated lighting to create a striking (if scarcely rural) effect at night. It also had one of the largest cinema car parks in the country, with space for 600 cars and a large number of cycles. The cinema was taken over by the ABC chain in the 1960s and eventually closed in December 1971. Brassey House, the block of shops and flats beyond, was named after A. Brassey Taylor, part owner of the Ashley Park estate, who built it in 1936.

THE REGAL CINEMA c.1938

The Regal was opened on 26th March, 1938, by Commander Arthur Marsden, R.N., M.P. for the Chertsey Division. Its founder-Manager was Clifford Spain, who had left the Capitol to open the new cinema, reckoned one of the most modern in the country. The programme on the first night included the film "Wife, Doctor and Nurse", the Kneller Band and Fanfare Trumpeters and Reginald Foort, who came from the B.B.C. to christen the £4,000 Compton organ. This, an exact replica of the B.B.C. theatre organ, had a console mounted on a lift in the orchestra pit. In the auditorium, all 2,000 seats were given generous spacing and an uninterrupted view of the screen. The ceiling was finished in metallic silver with indirect lighting, while the walls were decorated in metallic gold and rust brown. The latest R.C.A. projection apparatus and sound system were installed. Prices ranged from 6d (2½p) in the front stalls for a matinee to 3s.6d (17½p) in the front circle after 2.30 p.m. The Regal was the only Walton cinema with a restaurant, where in 1938 a four-course luncheon cost 1s.9d (approx. 9p).

THE NETTLEFOLD STUDIOS c.1950

In 1899 Cecil Hepworth rented for £36 p.a. a small house in Hurst Grove, where he began to make moving pictures on a stage in the garden. Outdoor scenes were shot in Walton using local buildings. At first he was totally dependent on daylight, but after a few years he erected his first studio, seen here near the bottom right behind the houses on the corner of Bridge Street and Hurst Grove. Hepworth Picture Plays Ltd. closed down in 1923 and a few years later the studios were purchased by Archibald Nettlefold Productions, which made films and television programmes here until 1961, after which the site was purchased by a development company who, in co-operation with the Council, built Hepworth Way and the present shopping centre on this and adjacent land. This photograph by Aerofilms shows at the bottom left "The Croft" in Bridge Street, a former convent which became the studio offices. The large building in the centre is the main stage, with a smaller stage to the right between it and the houses on the left of Hurst Grove. Just beyond these houses is the canteen. The houses on the right of the road were masked out by trees when the photograph was retouched for publicity purposes.

THE NETTLEFOLD STUDIOS 1959

By 1919 the British film industry had fallen behind many of its foreign competitors, notably in America, which had been able to continue developing during the War years. In an effort to rectify this situation, Archibald Nettlefold visited Hollywood in 1929 to study American production methods. A new theatre was built at Hurst Grove, the latest recording equipment installed, and other alterations made which enabled Nettlefold's to improve the quality of their productions and compete on more equal terms. The studios were nevertheless criticised for their small size, and this photograph shows the typical crowded conditions with actors, production staff and equipment crammed into a surprisingly limited space. The set is the court room used in "Oscar Wilde", released in 1959, which starred Ralph Richardson, Phyllis Calvert, Dennis Price and Robert Morley.

THE "OLD TIMES" COACH, BRIDGE STREET, 1890

Photographer Thomas Griffin of Weybridge stood on the forecourt of The Bear Inn to record the return from Ascot of the "Old Times" coach in June 1890. The house seen behind the coach is Cypress Lodge, which stood opposite The Bear near the Old Cottage teashop, on the site of the 1930s shops numbered 33-41 Bridge Street. The projecting porch of the house was decorated with stained glass. At this date it was occupied by Walter Key, but in the first decade of the present century it was acquired by Robert Foote, whose father, Samuel, lived nearby at Orchard House, on the site of the present Orchard Court. Samuel Foote, originally a gardener, had made his fortune as a bookmaker and owner of two or three London pubs.

THE BEAR INN AND BRIDGE STREET, c.1915

The Bear Inn, on the left, which was rebuilt in its present form within a few years of the taking of this photograph, has been trading since at least 1729. In the early 20th century it was patronised at lunchtimes by actors and technicians from Hepworth's Studios, and was popular with the "beanfeasters" who came to Walton on day-trips from London. It was also favoured by a travelling showman who made occasional visits to Walton with a performing bear. The bear would be kept overnight in the inn stables, and the horses remained very restless until the animal's scent wore off some days after its departure. In 1915 the landlord was Henry James Nightingale. The cart outside has travelled from Suffolk Wharf, Camden Town. In the distance, near the corner of Thames Street, is the shop of William Waldock, men's hairdresser.

BRIDGE STREET LOOKING WEST c.1920
Narrow though it seems to us now, in the 1920s this was still the main road from the centre of Walton towards Walton Bridge and Oatlands. The elegant gas lamp on the right had formerly stood at the junction with Church Street until 1898, when it was removed to make way for a new drinking fountain. Behind it can be seen part of The George public house on the corner of Thames Street, probably established in the 1880s, and at this time run by James Morgan. W.H. Slade, here advertising "Photographers Day & Night", set up his "Olde Studio" at no. 24 after the First World War. It was taken over in the mid-1920s by his fellow photographer Harold Whittingham, formerly based in Terrace Road, who carried on the business here until he moved to 71a High Street c.1936. The garage on the left was run by J.W.A. Taylor.

4 BRIDGE STREET c.1937
Edmund Jordan had taken over the printing and stationery business at 4 Bridge Street, formerly known as "Phillipson's Library", around 1910, and initially ran a sub-post office here as well. In addition, he was involved with the local film industry and took many excellent photographs of Walton, some of which he published as postcards for sale in his shop. A collection of his original glass negatives, mainly dating to the 1930s, is housed at Elmbridge Museum, and prints from some of them are reproduced here. The shop was later sold to T.F. Taylor. He closed the shop soon after the outbreak of the Second World War and with his family returned to South Africa.

MILITARY FUNERAL, BRIDGE STREET, c.1917
Taken from an upper window of Annett's shop, this view of Bridge Street shows a column of British soldiers, possibly from a mounted unit, heading the funeral procession of one of the 17 New Zealand soldiers who are buried in Walton Cemetery. Some of his comrades march beside the horse-drawn hearse. The posters on the side wall of Stonebanks' Shipping Agency, on the left, echo the war theme. In front of it is a side door of the Duke's Head, and between Stonebanks' and the coachbuilding works run by the three Wheatley brothers is the shop of the German jeweller and clockmaker, Hermann Hilbrand. When the two sons of Mr. Seaby, a local cab driver, were killed in the war, his wife stirred up a mob to attack Mr. Hilbrand's shop. The incident ended when Mr. Keswick, M.P. for Walton, read the Riot Act at the junction of Church Street from the roof of the horse bus in which he and some extra policemen had just arrived from Chertsey.

THE DUKE'S HEAD c.1878
The earliest known reference to the Duke's Head is in 1792. Evidence found during its demolition in 1970 suggests that it had been built only a year or two before, but an earlier inn may have stood on the site previously. The couple standing outside the door are no doubt the landlord, William Gale, and his wife Sarah. In the early 1900s, the inn is said to have been a favourite place for commercial travellers needing to stay in Walton overnight. There was a skittle alley at the end of the garden, which was used for a few years after 1918 as the meeting place of the Ashley Park Lodge of Oddfellows. The games played in the local hostelries did not always meet with the approval of the authorities: in February 1913, Supt. Marshall of Hersham reported that "the game of darts was being extensively played in the Walton district, and he had found it necessary to give notice to the publicans to put a stop to the practice." The inn closed in December 1966 when the present Duke's Head opened in Hepworth Way. The site is now occupied by Woolworth's.

BRIDGE STREET JUNCTION c.1900

This view clearly illustrates the awkward 16-foot-wide entrance to Bridge Street, known at this time as "Annett's Corner". Carts took the corner with considerable caution, and as early as 1901 children were warned to take care crossing here! Early in 1909 a 10 m.p.h. speed limit was imposed at this point in an attempt to reduce the risk of accidents, particularly in view of the increase in motor traffic. On the left is the china shop run by Miss Annett, sister of the local builders. The shop was still trading under the same name in 1938. Beyond it is the Duke's Head, now run by Charles Davey. John Bristow's furniture shop, which faced the High Street, had been in operation since the 1880s.

MAYO ROAD c.1910

Still open fields during the latter part of the 19th century, the area to the north of Thames Street was bought up by the brothers Harry Mayo and Harvey Dale, who owned the butcher's shop facing the end of Church Street. They also farmed Lonesome Farm, Crown Farm and Fishmore Farm, and initially used this land as additional pasture for their cattle. By the mid-1890s the north side of Thames Street had been built up and a row of houses was appearing on the east side of Vicarage Walk, which ran along the edge of the fields. The brothers progressively developed the remainder of the area to create Harvey Road and Dale Road, while this part of Vicarage Walk, now considerably widened, was renamed Mayo Road. The reason for the unusual position of the gas lamp in the carriageway is not clear, but perhaps it was a relic of the days when Vicarage Walk had been a mere footpath with a few houses on one side.

THE MANOR HOUSE INTERIOR, c.1910

The southern end of the long central hall was plainly photographed by Harold Whittingham while it was in the course of reconstruction. The temporary absence of the staircase to the gallery allows an uninterrupted view of the doors leading to the two rooms on the ground floor of the south wing. Above, the original roof structure with its king-posts and tie beams, now hidden by a false ceiling installed to conserve heat, is still open to view as it would have been when first built. The large brick fireplace on the right was subsequently reduced in size by the construction of a smaller one inside it. Note the pair of iron fire-dogs in the hearth, which would have supported a log fire.

HEPWORTH EXTRAS, 1914-15

Gathered in front of The Old Manor House public house are part of the cast of "Barnaby Rudge", released in January 1915. Most of the 1,500 people in the film would have been local residents employed as extras. In his publicity material, Hepworth claimed to have reconstructed "Entire streets in exact replica of Old London", but this photograph was evidently taken during a break in filming - hence the children in contemporary dress with the bicycle. A former local resident states that "They did most of the Dickens films in a little alley-way next to the Manor Pub. They were tiny Dickens-type cottages and the money the occupants got, paid for their winter coal and rent." The film's director, Thomas Bentley, had already made silent film versions of three other Dickens novels for Hepworth. This one, based on Dickens' story set at the time of the Gordon Riots in the late 18th century, ran for 1 hour 43 minutes. The first licence for The Old Manor House was granted in 1866 to local fisherman John Rosewell, whose son John Thomas Sedgwick Rosewell had taken over by 1887. By 1915 the pub was run by Frederick Broomfield.

THE SWAN HOTEL, 1911

The local drag hunt is shown here meeting outside The Swan early in 1911. As can be seen, many of the followers were on foot, although a report of a meet at Ashley Park in February 1913 records a good "field" of 30 mounted ladies and gentlemen. Louise Bale, whose father took over the hotel in 1911, recalls these meets outside: "A man would go ahead to carry the scent along the trail which was across all the towing path side meadows down to Sunbury Lock." The Swan was also popular with cyclists and had a large boating clientéle, as it had an attractive garden sloping down to the river and its own landing stage. There had been a small inn or alehouse on this site since at least 1769, but the present building evidently dates to the late 1870s, as it was described in January 1880 as "an entirely new building".

THE SWAN HOTEL 1923

This interior shot shows the bar in the Tap Room. This room was equipped for crib, dominoes, shove-halfpenny and darts. Another regular form of entertainment was a sing-song around the piano after closing time on Saturday night. As was usual, it also had sawdust on the floor and spittoons for the customers' use. A large flagon of R. White's ginger beer stands prominently on the bar beneath the gas light which was still in use at this date. The hotel also had a public bar, a private bar and a lounge. Its catering had a good reputation, and many of Hepworth's film stars would come here for meals. Lunch cost 2s. 6d. (12½p), while bed and breakfast was 7s. 6d. (37½p). Two of Hepworth's stars, Stewart Rome (who later went to Hollywood) and Lionel Howard, lived at The Swan for several years. The hotel, especially the porch and garden, and Miss Bale and her father, all appeared in Hepworth's films on occasion, and the bar furniture was frequently borrowed for the day!

WALTON'S FIRST BROWNIES, 1922

The 1st Walton St. Mary's Guides and Brownies were set up in 1921, many of the members being drawn from the church's Sunday School. During the First World War, Girl Guides from neighbouring towns had helped in various local war hospitals, and this had no doubt fed enthusiasm for the movement and helped to create a demand for a company in Walton, and also for a similar group for younger girls. The brownies pictured here in the Vicarage garden are, from left to right:

Back row (standing): Gwen Annear, Joy Godfrey, Mabel Covington, Amy Player (Assistant), Linda Godfrey, Alice Jordan, Florrie Godfrey, Sylvia Shepherd, Muriel Wright, Grace Atkins, Ethel Paul (Assistant), ?, Phyllis Harding, Florrie Holloway.
2nd row: Daphne Berridge, Florrie Martin(?), Miss Mary Hayes (Tawny Owl), Miss Edith Andrews (Brown Owl), Gladys Berridge(?), ?, Grace Atkins.
3rd row: Freda Saunders, Agnes Tivey, ?, Winnie Stenning, Mollie Naish, ?, Olive Ewen, Joan Saunders, Eileen Naish, Betty Berridge, Gladys Leggett.
Front row: Peggy Saunders, Eileen Remnant, Jessie Cosson, Doris Smart, Dorothy Coleman, ?, ?, Kathleen Sedgeley.

ST. MARY'S CHURCH AND VICARAGE c.1930

Although the house off Terrace Road later known as Walton Grove, demolished in 1973, was known until the 1860s as "The Parsonage", it ceased to serve this purpose when the rectorial rights passed to York Minster in 1413. Thereafter, the care of the parish was delegated to vicars. A vicarage may well have been built shortly after that date and one was certainly in existence by 1705. The building of which part is shown here on the left appears to have been in existence by 1800. As can be seen, the old vicarage was very conveniently situated between the churchyard and the former vicarage orchard consecrated as a burial ground in 1895. The vicarage remained in use until late 1938, when a new one on the Ashley Park estate was completed. The house was then demolished and replaced by the flats known as Regnolruf Court.

ST. MARY'S CHURCH c.1911

A postcard published by Harold Smith, stationer and draper, of 5, High Street, shows the interior of St. Mary's c.1911, the centre of the picture being dominated by one of the two magnificent brass chandeliers which then hung in the church. Gas light had replaced the candles formerly used to light the building in 1865, but electric lighting was not installed until 1935. Behind the chandelier is the 14th-century chancel arch, on which some restoration work was carried out in 1912. On the extreme left is the Shannon Memorial, executed by the French sculptor Louis François Roubiliac c.1758 in memory of Field-Marshal Richard Boyle, Viscount Shannon, of Ashley House, who died in 1740. The wooden gallery over the south aisle on the right, erected in 1765, was removed in July 1924, the normal daily services being suspended for a week while the work was in progress. The demolition was part of alterations to create the new War Memorial Baptistry in the south-west corner of the church.

CHURCH STREET AND TERRACE ROAD c.1925

The north-eastern end of Church Street at this point has seen considerable changes since this photograph was taken. The Castle inn, apparently established about 1740, stood just opposite the churchyard gate and was in the ownership of the Isleworth Brewery from 1886 to 1924, when the brewery was taken over by Watney Combe Reid & Co. Ltd. The prominent building beyond was Blake's drapery and furnishing shop, said to have been "more like an emporium". Joseph Blake, draper and silk mercer, had opened a shop on this site in 1843, but it was rebuilt as seen here in 1903-4. It was destroyed by incendiary bombs in the raid which damaged the church on 14th March, 1944, when the roof of The Castle was also badly damaged and subsequently replaced by a flat roof. The inn, however, continued to trade until Easter 1972. It was demolished in February 1973. The Methodist chapel in Terrace Road can be seen in the distance.

C.F. ANNEAR'S SHOP 1909

Charles F. Annear opened his grocer's shop at 35 Church Street between 1900 and 1908 and was trading here until the 1940s. The man shown standing in the doorway is believed to be William Wheatley, who later remembered making deliveries to the tenements in the Old Manor House, and to the fair which visited Cowey each year. A 14-year-old who started work at a nearby grocer's in 1908 recalled many years later that his employer's shop was open from 8 a.m. to 8 p.m., with late opening until 9 p.m. on Friday and 10 p.m. on Saturday, and early closing at 1 p.m. on Wednesday. Allowing for lunch and tea breaks, he worked 60½ hours per week, for which he was paid 4s (20p)! A sign displayed in the shop announced that, under the Shops Act, "young persons" were not permitted to work more than 74 hours per week. Most goods were delivered in bulk and had to be weighed out and wrapped for customers. In the case of flour, the whole shop was shrouded in dust sheets and enough packaged to last several weeks, after which the premises still had to be thoroughly dusted. A 3½ lb. bag of flour cost 6d (2½p), while the Cadbury's cocoa advertised on Mr. Annear's door was 5½d per ¼ lb.

CHURCH STREET LOOKING SOUTH WEST c.1915

This photograph illustrates the wide range of shops to be found in an average shopping street 70 years ago. The building on the left with the projecting frontage was occupied by John Seaby, a jobmaster and fly proprietor (the forerunner of the modern taxi company), while Mrs. E. Seaby ran the tearooms on the extreme left. When Mr. Seaby was ill, his wife would don his clothes, including a top hat and long boots, and take his place as driver. Between their two premises was the shop of F. Hopkins, florist and fruiterer. Arthur Bailey had been running his draper's shop since the 1890s. On the right, Charles Hemmings, innkeeper at The Castle since about 1880, was to hold the licence until the mid-1930s. Beyond Annear's grocer's shop is C. Oram's antique furniture shop, while the frame of the former White Hart inn sign now holds an estate agent's sign.

WHITE HART INN AND CHURCH STREET, 1902

This picture, taken when the street was patriotically decorated for the coronation of Edward VII on 8th August, 1902, shows on the right the old White Hart inn, which closed at about this time. The inn, now shops numbered 23-27 Church Street, was Walton's oldest surviving public house, known to have been operating at least as early as the 1660s, when it was known as the White Lion. A severe shortage of small change during that period induced many traders to issue their own "token" currency, and Charles Erwin, the innkeeper here, produced a half-penny token. The archway leading to the inn yard can be seen at the far end of the building.

CHURCH STREET LOOKING NORTH EAST c.1937

During the years before the outbreak of the Second World War, it was still possible for Edmund Jordan to stand in the middle of Church Street in order to record this scene. On the left, just beyond Robert Knight's newsagent's shop, is the former White Hart, now occupied by a snack bar belonging to Roy Wood (formerly a greengrocer), B. Solly's fish shop (still trading in 1994) and Vincent's cycle agent's, run by V.H. Smith. The archway formerly leading to the inn yard was now the entrance to the Working Men's Club, which had had its home here for many years. In December 1912 the "Surrey Herald" had commented on the improvements carried out there during the year, including the addition of a concert room and a bowling green. On the right an aproned butcher, possibly the proprietor, John Harry Ridge, is talking to a customer outside his shop. The premises beyond were in the occupation of W. Ward, cabinet maker, and Arthur Snell, draper.

CHURCH STREET 1916

Taken in April 1916, this photograph shows a Sopwith Gunbus being transported along Church Street, possibly coming from Brooklands. These aeroplanes, of which only six were built by Robey's of Lincolnshire in late 1915, were powered by 150 h.p. Sunbeam engines. The gunbus was a "pusher"; the rear-facing engine and four-bladed propeller being mounted behind the tandem cockpit arrangement. Unfortunately, probably because of war-time reporting restrictions, the reason for the machine's journey through Walton remains obscure. Behind it is Love & Sons' Garage, formerly a large grocer's shop run for 13 years by Mr. C.T. Hirst, and after his retirement in 1907 by Vernon Burton. A little further along, beyond the 17th century building still named after Admiral Rodney, whose family lived in Walton, is the Palace Cinema. This establishment was run by Arthur W. Love, previously manager of the Picture Palace in the Village Hall. Built in 1915, the Palace - later renamed the Regent - was Walton's first purpose-built cinema. In the foreground is the drinking fountain, surrounded by the railings erected in 1906 to protect it from the vandalism of the local children.

PEACE CELEBRATIONS, 19TH JULY, 1919

Walton's official celebrations at the end of the First World War began in the morning with a procession including decorated vehicles, cycles and individuals in fancy dress. The procession was headed by the Walton Drum and Fife Band. Also included were soldiers, demobilised men, boy scouts, the V.A.D. men's section and members of various societies. Starting from Halfway Green, the procession travelled along Hersham Road, High Street, Bridge Street, Manor Road and back to the fountain in Church Street, where addresses were given by Cllr. Miskin and Cllr. Phillips. Harold Whittingham recorded this scene as the last of the procession gathered for the speeches. In the afternoon, a short service attended by local schoolchildren was held in the same spot, followed by games and sports in Ashley Park and tea for children and residents aged over 70. The evening was enlivened by a dance in the Church Hall, a bonfire near the fountain, firework displays and the illuminations with which local people had decorated houses, business premises and boats.

W.E.BIRKHEAD'S SHOP c.1930

William and Charles Giles were in business as harness-makers at 24 Church Street in 1845, and it is said that the business was established in 1750. By 1887 the shop was under the direction of Mrs. Mary Giles, and the Birkhead family bought the business in 1890, running it with a staff of four. Its character gradually changed, and by 1915 William Edgar Birkhead was describing himself as a cycle maker, although the saddlery business was still carried on alongside this. In the 1930s, sports goods became an important part of the stock. The firm became a limited company in 1939. By 1972, the little saddler's shop had grown into a department store with a staff of 40, selling radio and television sets, electrical goods, hardware, sports and leisure equipment, leather goods, baby clothes and nursery equipment, and kitchen units. The shop was demolished a few years later.

CHURCH STREET c.1915

Two motorcyclists have stopped to consult their map outside the "Surrey Herald" printing works, the Walton branch of which had been established at 39 High Street c.1887. When the lease expired in 1905, they moved to "more commodious premises" at the upper end of the High Street where they remained for several years before moving again to the former Post Office building shown here. Next door is The Dolphin off licence, and beyond this a row of three shops built c.1902-3 to replace some small white-fronted shops. They were occupied by Merrick's Dairy, Adam Charles Bell's men's outfitters, and a jeweller's shop. A.C. Bell took over his shop, formerly run by Mr. Collier, on 15th May, 1907, the stock and debts being valued at £455.12s.02d and the lease, fixtures and goodwill at £175. The management of the business passed to his son and daughter-in-law, Roland and Phyllis Bell, in 1932, and to their two daughters in the early 1960s. It closed in 1974 and was demolished to make way for Barclay's Bank.

CHURCH STREET c.1935

Taken about 20 years later, this view by Edmund Jordan shows the former "Surrey Herald" premises now divided into two shops occupied by Kidman & Co., estate agents, and Eugénie Barnes, ladies' costumier and milliner. Merrick's Dairy is now The Café, taken over at about this date by Mrs. Burnett. The drinking fountain, removed to the Elm Grove Recreation Ground in 1930 after the lamp and direction sign on top were damaged by a gale, has been replaced by an electric lamp standard. The road surface below it has now been painted with "white lines", first used by Walton U.D.C. in 1925, giving the scene a more modern appearance.

HIGH STREET AREA c.1925

This aerial view, photographed by Surrey Flying Services of Croydon, shows the area later transformed by the construction of New Zealand Avenue in 1933. The new road was to join the High Street north of the Ashley Road School on the site of the old pound (seen here as a small dark square opposite the tip of the triangular green by the War Memorial). The development of the western side of the High Street is already well under way. Part of Church Street is visible at the top left, while the Amalgamated Dental factory, now with buildings on both sides of Churchfield Road, is clearly shown near the centre of the picture. As can be seen, both Churchfield and Winchester Roads were now almost completely developed as far as Esher Avenue. Elm Grove, at this time the offices of the Walton Urban District Council, can be seen on the right.

THE DOLPHIN c.1925

The history of The Dolphin is as yet little known and is worthy of further research, but it seems likely that William King in 1887, Alexander Adam Strachan in 1895 and George Sharp in 1899 - all beer retailers in Church Street - were in fact licensees of this little beer house. A contemporary plan in Elmbridge Museum confirms that it was trading as a beerhouse by 1899, and it continued as such into the first years of this century. It was, however, affected by the progressive tightening of the licensing laws during the years leading up to the First World War, and at the Licensing Sessions of 1907 it was decided that it was unsuitable for an on-licence, but it was granted a full off-licence. A photograph of 1909 in Walton Library shows the premises with the name "Andrew" above the window, and Kelly's Directory of 1911 lists Henry Thomas Andrew as the proprietor of a restaurant in Church Street. By 1915, the Dolphin had passed into the hands of Benjamin Harry Wood, and he and, later, his widow Minnie, were to run the business until c.1940. It remained an off-license until at least 1950. The accompanying photograph shows The Dolphin's Trojan van, used for deliveries to customers' homes. A free delivery service was general at this period, when few customers had their own transport.

"RAIDING THE BANK", CHURCH STREET, 1909

A popular form of free entertainment in Walton at the beginning of the 20th century was watching the filming of Cecil Hepworth's films. Local people were also frequently required to act as "extras" for a small fee. Here, a ten-minute film entitled "An Attempt to Smash a Bank" is in course of production - the improbably named "London & N.E. Bank" being, in fact, the former Post Office, recently replaced by the new building in Hersham Road. The plot was about a rich man who, spurned by the banker's daughter, withdrew all his money and caused a run on the bank. The film was directed by the Dutchman Theo Bouwmeester, and is one of only two survivors of the 49 films which he made for Hepworth. For some years, Hepworth regularly used locations in the town as his sets. Unfortunately, filming was only possible while the sun was shining, and the traffic was often held up until weather conditions allowed the crew to finish the scene. Eventually the authorities put a stop to this practice, but by that time Hepworth had built his first studio, allowing him to film indoors. Richard Julius Bittdorf, whose name appears on the front of the Crown Hotel, had in fact died in March 1906, at the age of 45, after only six months as landlord. His widow, however, may well have taken over the licence.

J. IVE & CO. c.1905-1910

Henry Dale & Co.'s shop, "easily the biggest butcher in the village" in 1900, had passed into the hands of Mr. J. Ive by December 1906, when the "Surrey Herald" mentions "Messrs. Ive's great show where serried ranks of beasts for Christmas fare provide a tempting spectacle". Mr. Ive had extended the canopy of the shop to facilitate these impressive displays. The animals were slaughtered at the bottom of the yard behind the shop, normally in the afternoons when most of the deliveries had been completed for the day. The proceedings were often watched by the local boys, who would take turns to peer through a small gap in the gate beside the shop until they were chased off! These premises, facing down Church Street, were to remain a butcher's shop under J.E. Grimditch until the building was demolished c.1963.

TURNER'S CYCLE SHOP c.1916 and 1900

George Turner came to Walton-on-Thames around 1870 and started his cycle works in 1889, producing the Walton Cycle here from about 1900. During the First World War, the soldiers convalescing at the New Zealand Hospital in Mount Felix would hire cycles here in order to explore the neighbourhood. Rickshaws like the one in the foreground of the interior view were particularly useful for those not yet able to pedal their own bicycle. Like many cycle shops, Turner's took to repairing motor cycles and cars, which eventually became their principal trade. They also branched out into the radio business and were already selling phonographs and cylinder records in about 1905. By the 1930s they had a radio shop adjacent to the garage. The business remained in the family until 1963, when the building was demolished for the construction of Hepworth Way.

CROWN HOTEL AND HIGH STREET c.1935
Occupying a prime situation on the corner of Church Street and High Street, the Crown Hotel had been in business since at least 1729, when the licensee was Joseph Goodchild. The building itself was older, being of 16th-century construction behind the late 17th- or early 18th-century facade and later ground-floor extension. In 1935, the landlord was Mr. J.E. Butt. The pub was demolished in 1961 and shops built on the site. On the far side of the High Street, J. Ive's shop had been taken over by J.E. Grimditch, but his predecessor's name remained in place in the roof tiles and on the shop front below the windows. Further along, the high brick wall and overhanging trees of Ashley Park had by this time been entirely replaced by the shops erected in the late 1920s.

HIGH STREET LOOKING SOUTH c.1910
This view by Harold Whittingham shows the north end of the High Street some 25 years earlier. Whittingham had left royal photographers J. Russell & Sons of Baker Street, London, to open his own studio in Terrace Road in October 1907. In the left foreground is Ainslie Brothers' butcher's shop. This business survived for many years in spite of its close proximity to Mr. Ive's much larger shop. At a time when most shops were small family businesses, it was usual for several competing traders to flourish in the same street.

HIGH STREET LOOKING NORTH c.1910

Looking towards the Duke's Head and Crown Inns, we see a dray belonging to Isleworth Breweries passing the premises of car dealer H. Garrat. The lady with the bicycle is outside the shop of Edward Power & Son, Chemists and Druggists, where local people needing a doctor to call could leave him a message, often saving themselves a long walk to his house. In the mid-1880s Mr. Power's eldest son, Edward, who had been apprenticed to an instrument maker, set up with his two brothers a business making dental instruments in a shed behind the shop. One brother, Thomas Henry, also practised as a dentist until about 1922. They marketed their products through Claudius Ash of London, and Power's instruments soon earned a reputation for excellence. The instruments were taken to Walton Station each morning on a handcart for despatch to London. By 1896 they had built a factory in Church Walk, on a site south of Churchfield Road. Beyond Power's shop can be seen Harold Smith's emporium, R.J. Stowe's shoe shop and Ainslie Brothers' butchers.

HIGH STREET LOOKING NORTH c.1955

This view, taken about 45 years later from a little further south, shows some obvious changes. The former Bristow's second-hand furniture shop on the corner of Church Street and Bridge Street has been replaced by the much larger building housing Doreen's fashion shop and, although the photograph shows little traffic, it was busy enough at times to necessitate the use of the pedestrian crossing. The former premises of Power & Son, still a chemist (Savory & Moore), and the shops beyond are little changed, but those opposite and in the right foreground date to the late 1920s. Coppen Bros. grocers, Woolworth's and Boots replace the old shops opposite the now-vanished Ashley Park gate.

HIGH STREET AND CHURCHFIELD ROAD CORNER, 1913

Pictured in the summer of 1913, this scene is dominated by the recently-redecorated premises of Timothy White, the chemist, who had taken a lease of the shop in January of that year, and were to remain there until they moved across the road in 1931. It had previously been occupied by a clothier, Frederick Field. Until December 1905 the "Surrey Herald" printing office had stood on the site. The building shown is now a Kentucky Fried Chicken take-away. On the near corner of Churchfield Road can be seen part of the old Village Hall. Among the group outside is a boy with two bottles of milk carefully packed in the basket of his bike. This was still something of a rarity, as most people bought their milk straight from the churn, decanting it into their own jugs. On the extreme left, next to the gas lamp, is an early speed limit sign. The first 10 m.p.h. speed limits in Walton were imposed in 1903 in an attempt to counter the "motor menace". At a meeting in February 1913, Walton Council had discussed their anxiety over the increasing cost of road maintenance - "they knew to their cost what heavy motor traffic had done for them...". The Council's expenditure on roads had more than doubled since 1902, from £1,983 to £5,300.

COURT'S FURNITURE SHOP, 1960

In about 1880, on the occasion of his marriage, Joseph Sassoon of Ashley Park gave the people of Walton a Village Hall. It was here, in 1894, that the elections for the first Walton Urban District Council were held. In the first decade of this century the room in the front of the building was a library run by Miss Warner. Film shows were also sometimes screened here, including some of Hepworth's early productions, and for some years prior to the opening in 1915 of the Palace Cinema in Church Street, the hall became Walton's first "Picture Palace". By 1922 it had become the motor showrooms of Love & Sons, who used the premises until the early 1930s, when it passed into the hands of builders' merchants Wiggins-Sankey. The shop later became Courts' furniture shop, and is shown here in 1960, shortly before they vacated the building, which subsequently became Tesco's. It is now the Superdrug store.

ROAD WIDENING, HIGH STREET, 1930

In 1924 the wall and trees marking the eastern boundary of Ashley Park had been taken down to enable the Council to widen the High Street. This was followed over the next few years by the building of shops, such as those illustrated on the left, along this side of the street. This photograph, taken only six years after the original work, shows further road widening in progress. In marked contrast to views taken twenty years earlier, the only horses in this busy street scene are those being used in the road works. On the left, at no. 46a, is Walton Fruit and Vegetable Market, and beyond it are the cleaners and dyers Achille Serre, Anne-Marie's Gowns, the Eight Hour dry cleaners, A. Marshall's tailor's shop, the Thames Book Shop and Freeman, Hardy and Willis' shoe shop.

WALTON-ON-THAMES
This map is reproduced from the 6 in. Ordnance Survey map of 1919/20

WALTON UPON THAMES

47 HIGH STREET 1916

The staff of J.J. Reading's fishmonger's pose outside the shop with its impressive display of Christmas poultry in December 1916. Second from the left is the Manager, Mr. Thomas Purdue, with his wife Annie beside him. The boy in the centre is Bernard Alfred Deakin, aged 14, and on the right next to the older shop boy are Mr. Purdue's daughter Winnie and his brother Henry. The shop, subsequently to become Mac Fisheries, and later Smith's Motor Accessories, was situated in the building with the distinctive Dutch gable, commonly known as "Ireton's House". Although it is probably of 17th century date, there seems to be no evidence that General Ireton ever actually lived here.

T. PURDUE'S DELIVERY TRICYCLE c.1911

Thomas Purdue is seen again here on the left, proudly displaying his new delivery tricycle for the camera. His son Thomas Harry Purdue is seated on the tricycle, while Winnie stands behind it. Mr. Purdue had moved to Walton from Shepperton c.1900 to manage Reading's shop, formerly Wells' fishmongers, and remained in business there until the 1930s.

THE FIRE STATION c.1904

Walton's first manual fire pump was purchased by the Chertsey Rural Sanitary Authority in 1875/76, and in April 1876 the Walton Vestry gave permission for the old lock-up in the High Street to be used as a fire station. This stood a little to the north of the present Wellington public house and by the time of this photograph it had been altered and extended. Here, the Brigade's Captain, Walter Brind, who ran a shoe shop on the other side of the street, stands with some of his men by the old manual pump. In June 1906 Firemen Eddie, Creasy and Bell all needed treatment for injuries to their hands caused by the levers on the out-of-date machine during practice. At the back of the pump is a strainer used when pumping water from ponds, etc. In the doorway behind stands a hose cart. In April 1909, the Council agreed to look into the cost of connecting the Fire Brigade with the telephone system for the benefit of local subscribers. The Brigade operated on a voluntary basis, the men leaving their normal work when the alarm was sounded. Local tradesmen in the Brigade included, amongst others, W. Birkhead, saddler; Thomas Purdue, fishmonger; the Annett brothers, builders; and J. Turner, son of George Turner, the cycle manufacturer.

HIGH STREET LOOKING NORTH c.1950

The former "Builders' Arms" was rebuilt on a much larger scale in the early 1930s to take full advantage of its new prime position on the corner of New Zealand Avenue. It was later renamed "The Kiwi", either in honour of the New Zealand soldiers who had been nursed at Mount Felix during the First World War, or to reflect the name of the new road. In 1987 it changed its name again to "The Wellington", still maintaining the New Zealand theme. The National Provincial Bank had replaced F. Stanley's chimney sweep's and confectioner's shop at no. 55 in the mid-1930s, when Mr. Stanley transferred his sweep's business to Garden Road. Trigg's Dairy was taken over by United Dairies c.1930.

THE UNVEILING OF WALTON WAR MEMORIAL, 1921

On the afternoon of Sunday 10th July, 1921, an audience estimated at nearly 3,000 attended the unveiling of the memorial to the men of Walton Parish who had died in the 1914-1918 War. Of approximately 1,100 Walton men who had fought, the names of 130 dead were inscribed on bronze panels and mounted on the Portland stone monument. Although seats had been reserved for relatives of the fallen, most of the crowd had to stand in the full sun, where the temperature reached 128°F. This explains the unconventional headgear of some of the choir! The short service preceding the unveiling was led by the Wesleyan Minister, Rev. B. Stanley, and followed by speeches by Dr. Drabble, Chairman of the War Memorial Committee, and the Earl Beatty, who then performed the unveiling. Admiral Beatty praised Walton's contribution, referring to the spirit of Drake and Rodney. The ceremony ended with a dedicatory prayer by the Vicar, Rev. Kemp Bussell, the Last Post, played by Bugler A. Pollard of the 6th East Surrey Regt., and the National Anthem.

SOUTHERN HIGH STREET c.1912

Looking north from the southern end of the High Street, the former Ashby's Bank, now Menzies, Chartered Accountants, stands in the left foreground with the old Builder's Arms tavern beyond. On the right beyond Winchester Road is a row of four shops built about 1890 on the site of William Reed's farm. Winchester Road itself was constructed not long afterwards, and in the later 1890s the row of shops named The Broadway, shown in the right foreground, replaced a villa named Colby House.

F. WOOD & CO'S SHOP c.1925
No. 85 High Street, known as Osborne House, was occupied by a succession of long-established grocers. The "Surrey Herald" of 17th October, 1913, reported that the late E.T. Madeley's shop had been sold to Mr. Fred Wood, "who has had high-class experience at Hastings and Herne Bay." Madeley had originally set up his business in Chertsey in the late 1860s, later acquiring additional premises in neighbouring towns, including Walton and Weybridge. This shop was much the largest grocer's in Walton, and served nearly all the large houses in the neighbourhood. As can be seen, Wood's shop, like many large grocers, by this time boasted a Renault delivery van, although this would no doubt have been supplemented by the use of delivery boys on bikes. Wood remained in business here until at least the late 1930s, the shop later being taken over by the Co-op, and eventually demolished.

LIBRARY AND HIGH STREET c.1935
In 1827 a plot of land on the site of the present library was acquired for the purpose of building a new National School. In 1858 the older children were moved to the new school at the north end of Ashley Road and the old premises became the Infants' School. This was rebuilt in its present form in 1884. The school moved to a new building in Ambleside Avenue in 1931 and the old school became a Labour Exchange. The Public Library, first opened in the Walton Women's Club in 1924, had for some years been housed in one room at Elm Grove and now handled an average weekly issue of 1,061 books. In 1933 it was moved to its present accommodation in the former infants' school. The old Capitol Cinema, on the right beyond the entrance to Elm Grove, became The Odeon after the end of the Second World War. The photograph was taken by Edmund Jordan of Bridge Street.

HIGH STREET AND HERSHAM ROAD, 1931

The Capitol Cinema is seen here with a "crashed German aeroplane" on its roof, advertising the film "Hell's Angels". The plane seems, in fact, to have the fuselage of a British civilian-registered aircraft, part of its registration being still faintly visible behind and beneath the German cross. It was probably made up of damaged parts obtained from the Brooklands airfield. The film "Hell's Angels", originally released as a silent movie in 1930 starring James Hall, Greta Nissen and Ben Lyon, was subsequently re-made as a "talkie" with Jean Harlow as the new leading lady. The new version was screened at the Capitol for six days from 28th September, 1931. While the plot was notoriously weak, the stunning flying sequences attracted large audiences. In his vision of the cinema of the future, published in 1930, Clifford Spain pictured a "building so extensive that we have on the roof a landing ground for patrons coming in by 'plane, one corner of which would be used for parking the 'planes." Perhaps this idea inspired his later bold publicity!

THE CAPITOL CINEMA
c.1928

The Capitol, the first large cinema in the area, opened on 30th December, 1927, only four-and-a-half months after building commenced. It was established by the London Cinema Director and owner, Mr. L. Morris, and its Manager until 1938 was the local cinema entrepreneur, Clifford Spain, who regarded the new building as "the last word in cinema construction". The Capitol was equipped with the latest in lighting, heating, ventilation, projection and seating, and boasted its own orchestra, the Capitol Players, headed by Mr. Clinch. These musicians accompanied the silent films screened here during the first two years of its existence. The first "talkies" were shown here in January 1930, after the installation of the "Western Electric Sound System", which had been selected by the Management as "the finest reproduction equipment available". After the Second World War, the cinema was taken over by the Odeon chain and continued under that name until its closure on 29th November, 1980. It was demolished in January/February 1981. The Screen Cinema now stands on a site close by.

INFANTS' SCHOOL c.1909

The photograph shows a typical classroom of 1909-10, with 40-50 children seated in rows at fixed desks. In the infants, boys and girls were mixed together as seen here, but their older brothers and sisters attended separate schools. Slates were used for the younger children when learning writing and arithmetic, but here they have been put away for a pottery lesson. One local man recalls his class being put into pairs so that the girls could teach the boys how to knit. The school was staffed at this time by the Headmistress, Mrs. A.E. Hisman, and four assistants, of whom only one had a teaching certificate. 1909 was a difficult year: the school was closed for several weeks from 24th May because of a measles epidemic. In addition, despite the opening of the East Walton School in 1908, the upper schools were so overcrowded that no children could be transferred from the infants.

ASHLEY ROAD, 1920s

At the junction of Ashley Road (formerly Common Road) and the High Street was the village pound, seen here as a short stretch of post and rail fencing. Attached to the posts were chains for securing animals. A local man who attended the Boys' School beyond from 1901 to 1906 later recalled: "The village had a pound which was next to the school playground, and occasionally we would see horses and cattle which had strayed and been "impounded". To release these animals the owner had to pay so much for each...". The old Walton Parochial School Mixed Department had been rebuilt on this site in 1858 and was enlarged in 1882. The same former pupil remembered that in his time "The urinals were out in the open air, whilst the WCs were cubicles with seats over a long trough which the school cleaner had to empty:...For drinking purposes we had one outside tap, by the side of which was a metal cup fastened to the wall by a stout chain...One cup to about 100 boys!" While the school is still in use, the pound was destroyed during the building of New Zealand Avenue.

THE PLOUGH INN 1909

The Plough, at the north end of Ashley Road where it joins the High Street, has been in operation since at least 1778, but the present building replaced that shown here in 1928. At the time of this photograph it was run by Mrs. Anne Butcher, whose husband Albert had been licensee from about 1887 until his death, aged 68, in September 1905. Prior to this, Mr. Butcher had appropriately kept a butcher's shop at Oatlands. Another example of Hepworth's use of local buildings in his films, the picture was taken during the shooting of "The Race for the Farmer's Cup" - a 725-ft. silent film lasting 11½ minutes and released in June 1909. The hero was a farmer who won the race and the girl in spite of his rival's attempt at sabotage. The part was played by the film's director, Lewin Fitzhamon (1869-1961), a former steeplechase jockey who used to act any part requiring a horseman and must have felt quite at home in this rôle.

ASHLEY PARK c.1908

Ashley House (known as Ashley Park from c.1800) was built in 1602-7 for Lady Jane Berkeley at a total cost of £3,119.4s.7½d. Extensive alterations and additions were carried out in the early 18th century by Sir Edward Lovett Pearce for Viscount Shannon, probably including the addition of the bow fronts to the east ends of the two wings. At the time of this photograph the owner was Joseph Sassoon (1855-1918), whose father had bought the house in the early 1860s. Joseph Sassoon sold off some land, and the "Surrey Herald" noted in December 1908 that development of the estate for building purposes had commenced during the year. The gates shown here opened on to Ashley Road. The Sassoon family reportedly preferred this entrance and seldom used the gates in the High Street. Following the death of Joseph Sassoon's son in 1922, the house and estate were sold by auction in 15 lots in April 1923 and the house demolished soon after. The estate was developed for housing.

THE HALL, ASHLEY PARK, c.1923

The hall and gallery in the centre of Ashley Park survived comparatively unaltered for over 300 years, although the windows seen here were probably installed in the 18th century. The original building accounts of 1602-1607 have survived and were published in 1977 by the Surrey Record Society as SRS Vol. XXIX, providing a fascinating insight into the materials, workmen and costs involved, and also into the sources of the materials. Some of the bricks were re-used materials from an old farmhouse which had stood nearby, the remainder coming from Egham, Botley, Chertsey, Esher, Isleworth and Kingston. Most of the wainscotting was purchased in London, but a local landowner, Mr. Inwood, supplied some of the board used, while again some came from the earlier house. One payment to the joiner of £10.13s.4d was for wainscotting the ends of the "great chamber", seen here, with "miter & sipher revayled, with 8 great carved pilosters with there petistalls, and the chymney peece". Supplies of 8"-square green and yellow paving tiles for the hall, porch and walk under the gallery were obtained from Warde the tileman of Chertsey (probably Ottershaw or Addlestone). A mid-17th-century staircase was dismantled and shipped to America when the house was demolished.

WALTON STATION c.1880 AND OCTOBER 1947

The London & Southampton Railway was opened from Nine Elms to Woking Common on 21st May, 1838. The following year it became the London & South Western Railway. Owing to local opposition, the station was built well away from the centre of Walton, and the Railway Company initially paid only £30 an acre for land here. Extensions of the line were opened to Southampton in 1840 and to Waterloo Bridge in 1848. Except between Nine Elms and Waterloo Bridge, the line originally consisted of two tracks, as shown in the earlier photograph, but the railway was widened in stages to four tracks, and Walton Station was rebuilt with a central platform c.1895. Originally known as Walton and Hersham, the station was renamed Walton-on-Thames in 1935, the year before the opening of Hersham Station. W.H. Smith first opened a bookstall at Walton Station on 5th August, 1872, and maintained this facility (a little to the left of the station name in the 1947 photograph) until 29th May, 1992. They have also had a shop in Walton since 1934. On the right of the later picture can be seen a group of milk churns awaiting collection - a common sight on railway platforms before the use of bulk road tankers.

STATION AVENUE c.1908

At a time when coal was still the principal means of heating, the bulk transport of this vital fuel was an important function of the railway system. This is reflected in the presence here of no less than three coal merchants' offices beside the station. Beyond them are the premises of auctioneers and estate agents Waring & Co. In the road stand three horse-drawn cabs. In December 1908 Messrs. Love & Co. applied to the Sanitary Committee for a licence for a motor car to ply for hire. This was granted, as were two drivers' licences for Harry and Ernest Love, subject to production of their Motor Drivers' Licences. This innovation spelt the beginning of the end for the horse cabs. In November 1912 the Council received a petition from the cabmen at Walton Station complaining that the new taxi cabs were allowed to stand and ply for hire on land forbidden to horse-cab drivers, giving the taxis an unfair advantage, but the Council's sympathetic response could not prevent the steady decline of their business.

KING GEORGE V IN STATION AVENUE, 1912

At 1.00 p.m. on Saturday, 11th May, 1912, King George V arrived at Walton by special train from Weymouth en route to Kempton Park. Having dressed for the race meeting, His Majesty was given a resounding welcome by the large crowd assembled outside the station as he walked to his waiting car. This was courteously acknowledged by the King, who then proceeded via Halfway through Walton to Sunbury. The occasion was recorded by local photographer and stationer R.J. Dubbin of Hersham Road, who subsequently took the opportunity of marketing the photograph as a postcard. The premises of Mrs. Elizabeth Parsons, delivery agent and contractor, are very conveniently situated close to the sidings where goods were loaded and unloaded. Mrs. Parsons was the widow of Charles Stephen Parsons, who had been in business here more than forty years before.

ASHLEY PARK HOTEL c.1907
Established in 1891, the Ashley Park Hotel was ideally placed to provide refreshment and accommodation for travellers using the nearby railway station. Transport between here and the centre of Walton was provided by horse-drawn bus or cab, but by the time this photograph was taken the landlord, Walter Shillitto, was already catering for travellers with cars, as evidenced by the Motor Garage offered on his sign. The poster on the tree behind the trap is advertising one of the village's annual regattas.

ASHLEY PARK HOTEL c.1927
Taken about 20 years after the previous photograph, this view shows the Hotel with a new, more urban image. The leafy surroundings have receded to the background and the formerly ivied walls have been given a fashionable half-timbered look, although structurally the building is little altered. The Ashley Garage now situated next door boasts no less than five brands of petrol, while H.W. Thornton's recently-opened "Kiosk" was a popular port of call for local children and no doubt also patronised by the hotel and station staff.

HALFWAY GREEN AND STATION AVENUE c.1908

A typical assortment of contemporary transport is represented on the road to the station. Motorised transport was still the exception, and it was quite usual to walk several miles to work or school. The large load of crates on the cart near the centre of the picture is no doubt to be despatched by train, while behind the cart is the bus which ran from the pump in Church Street to the Station. The service was inaugurated by Isaac Stowe c.1891. Mr. Stowe operated as a cab proprietor for about 30 years until his death in March 1909. The horses which pulled the bus were also used for the fire engine and when the alarm sounded they would be unharnessed and rushed to the Fire Station, leaving the passengers to continue their journey on foot. Another valuable means of communication at a time when telephones were still a comparative rarity was the telegraph boy seen in the foreground with his bike.

DANESFIELD SCHOOL c.1935

In the early 1920s Mrs. Constance Brabner of Danesfield, just north of the railway in Hersham Road, opened a private girls' boarding and day school following the death of her husband. The leopards seen here on the gateposts were given to the school c.1930, and adopted as the school badge. In 1932 a 25 per cent increase in pupils necessitated the building of a new dining hall for 150 children, additional classrooms and a kindergarten. Boys were admitted to the kindergarten and form 1. The school offered extensive sports facilities including a swimming pool, its own Companies of Guides, Brownies and Cubs, and a private bus service to surrounding districts. It was officially registered as a girls' public school c.1933. With the coming of the Second World War the Principal decided to close the school. Two Junior School teachers, Miss D. Quartermain and Miss A. Kaye, called a meeting of parents. In autumn 1940 the school re-opened at Rye House in Rydens Road, with Miss Quartermain and Miss Kaye as Principals. After the War the school moved again to its present site in Rydens Avenue. The original building shown here was demolished in the 1950s.

THE HALFWAY c.1907

All the buildings on the left in this view of Hersham Road are still standing, but modern shops and a garage have now replaced the three large houses - Woodlands, Bramlea and Danesfield - which stood behind the trees between the shops and the railway. In the foreground is part of Sillence's shop, now (1994) empty. Next to it is George William Prior's greengrocer's shop, trading from c.1890 to c.1930. These premises are now occupied by Pollington's newsagent's. For a short time around 1915, Mr. Prior also had a boot and shoe shop at 1, The Pavement, in the furthest parade of shops shown here, built c.1900. Next to the greengrocer's is Warren Bros. bakery, later Tilbury's and now Lee's Bakery. The four private houses beyond were soon to be converted for commercial use, and now house electronics and video shops, a pizza parlour and a sandwich bar.

THE HALFWAY, JUNE 1939

A later view of the Halfway shops, taken by a local resident, shows Trimby's draper's shop at no. 83 in the foreground. The shop was converted in 1880 from one of the original houses believed to have been built around the 1840s, and had been a draper's shop from that time. The original proprietors were Henry and Emily Mahon, but the Trimby sisters owned and ran the shop from 1896 to 1949. It was run thereafter by Mrs. Parker, and from 1960 until its closure early in 1994 by Mrs. H.J. Woods. Many of the original 1880s shop fittings survived until its closure and are now in the Elmbridge Museum collection. Next door is A. Jarvis & Sons' shop, a butcher's from at least 1898 (when the proprietor was James Merritt) until the recent closure of W.W. Meats. Mr. Blandford's radio shop is easily distinguishable just beyond. The front gardens of the four houses in the earlier photograph have all been replaced by projecting shop fronts, probably added by c.1915.

SILLENCE'S SHOP, THE HALFWAY, c.1905

The photographer C.W. Sillence took this photograph of his own shop at 89, Hersham Road and printed it as a postcard, written and posted by him in 1906. In the late 1890s the premises seem to have been occupied by Alfred James Gosden, photographer and stationer, and probably Sillence, who had another studio in Church Street, Weybridge, bought the establishment as a going concern. When Sillence emigrated to Canada in 1911 (possibly arranged through Stonebanks' Shipping Agency in Bridge Street), the business passed into the hands of R.J. Dubbin, another photographer and stationer, and then in the 1920s to George A. Blandford, also a stationer. By 1935, however, Mr. Blandford seems to have changed his trade, and the shop had become Blandford Radio. The photograph shows on the left an interesting assortment of Kodak products and on the right a display of Mr. Sillence's own photographic portraits. Hanging in the door are a selection of local picture postcard views for sale.

HALFWAY GREEN c.1937
The appearance of the eastern corner of the Halfway Green as seen from Station Avenue has changed little since the 1880s. The arrival of the railway in 1838 led to the development of the Halfway as a desirable residential area, and the shops on the left were built as houses in the 1840s. Prior to the opening of the new post office nearby in 1908, the shop on the corner of Rydens Road was an estate agent's and post office run by Edward Joseph Ingram and family, from whom the popular name "Ingram's Corner" derived. The Halfway House also owes its origin to the railway, having opened about 1838, and in the late 19th and early 20th century was called the Halfway House and Railway Tavern. It was threatened with closure in 1915 when the renewal of the licence was put back on account of the sanitary and structural condition of the premises, and subsequently renewed on condition that proposed alterations were carried out within 12 months. The landlord in the 1930s was Charles Moon. In 1991 the building was restyled and renamed "The Old Colonial Restaurant".

HALFWAY GREEN JUNE 1936
In contrast with the previous picture, these buildings along the eastern side of Halfway Green have all now disappeared. In 1935, however, all seven cottages were occupied, S. Lambeth was licensee of the Ashley Arms, and both the Halfway Garage and Allsops Garage were still in business. The Ashley Arms, with the cottage adjoining, was built about 1860, and it seems to have begun trading as a beer house around 1865. The pub was in private hands until 1902, when it was sold to the Isleworth Brewery Company. When the brewery went into liquidation in 1924, the Ashley Arms and the adjoining cottage were bought by Watney Combe Reid & Co. Ltd. for £1,485, but its former owners are recalled here, 12 years later, by the advertisement for Isleworth Ales & Stout. The Ashley Arms closed in 1993 and has now been demolished, together with the other surviving buildings. The site is currently being redeveloped.

THE ASHLEY ARMS CONCERT ROOM c.1905
This unusual photo by C.W. Sillence offers a glimpse of the entertainment to be found in local public houses before the First World War. A local man recalled that "The pubs provided wooden forms and tables with a sawdust covered floor, with spittoons very much in evidence!" The concert room seen here boasts the luxury of wooden chairs, although the bar was probably furnished with forms, and would have been open from 6 a.m. to serve men requiring a drink before work! The landlord, Alfred Joseph Wright, would have needed an entertainment licence if he wished to play the piano for his guests. No doubt he would also have had to light the two candles in the brackets if he needed to read the piano music, as the single light fitting must have provided somewhat inadequate illumination at night in a room full of smoking men. The identities of the men in the mural are unknown, although they were no doubt well known to contemporary customers, but the distinctive shapes of Walton Bridge and the model of Mount Felix are unmistakeable.

THE NEW POST OFFICE c.1910
Built in 1908 a little north of the Halfway shops, this "commodious Post Office" was considered by the "Surrey Herald" to be "a vast improvement on its predecessor, and far more in keeping with the requirements of the district," but although the last post in the evening was extended from 9.00 to 9.45 p.m., "in several respects the postal arrangements are justly regarded as being very unsatisfactory." The office had seven sub-post offices connected with it, and in 1909 the Postmaster was on a salary of £196 p.a. Working under him were four male and three female sorting clerks and telegraphists, one male trainee, five assistants and seventeen postmen. Differentials between the wages of male and female staff were marked: for example a male sorting clerk received between 15s (75p) and 43s (£2.15) per week, while a woman doing the same job would be paid from 12s (60p) to 24s (£1.20). The postman setting out on his bicycle could expect from 17s (85p) to 25s (£1.25) per week.

WALTON PARK NURSERIES, AUGUST 1946

Walton Park Nurseries were started by Horace Thompson in 1927, on a 40-acre site north of the railway on both sides of Molesey Road, Hersham. This imposing entrance was in Rydens Road, at the north end of the present Walton Park, while the other was on Molesey Road near Hersham Station. The nursery produced vegetables, soft fruit and salads, and a wide variety of garden plants, shrubs and fruit trees for sale. A big advertising campaign in 1931 also offered garden ornaments and stressed that customers could drive round the nurseries on a system of roads, with "no muddy walks". In spring 1984 the much-reduced nursery closed, the remaining 2½ acres being sold for housing, as the rest had been before. The firm, under Horace Thompson's grandson, Robert, planned to develop as a wholesale business on its land at Chobham.

RYDENS AVENUE c.1910

The name Rydens or "Roydens" means a clearing, and originally referred to a medieval common field occupying the area bounded by Rydens Road, Hersham Road and Molesey Road. Rydens Avenue is of much more recent origin, having been laid out in the late 19th century, and was still comparatively sparsely developed with housing in the 1930s.

WALTON COTTAGE HOSPITAL c.1907

A scheme was initiated in 1902 for commemorating the Coronation of Edward VII by building a cottage hospital in Walton. Dr. George White Drabble of Manor House, Church Street, gave freehold premises at the corner of Sidney Road and Rodney Road, the building was financed by appeals and the hospital furnished at the expense of Mr. Edward Pettitt. The foundation stone was laid by H.R.H. the Duchess of Albany on 28th May, 1904, and the Walton, Hersham and Oatlands Cottage Hospital opened on 13th June, 1905, with Dr. Drabble as Chairman and Miss R. MacAndrew as Matron. The building had beds for ten patients, who shared a bath and two lavatories. It was soon found, however, that the one bedroom provided for the nurses was inadequate, and one of the private wards had to be appropriated. The Management Committee therefore decided in September 1905 to extend the accommodation at a cost of £120. The resulting extra room can be seen here on the first floor at the left. The other first-floor bedrooms are for the nurses, servants and Matron. In 1906 the hospital treated 117 in-patients and 16 out-patients and carried out 40 operations. The original building shown here was demolished in 1993.

RODNEY HOUSE c.1928

Walton's first maternity home, in Rodney Road, is seen here, probably soon after its opening on 24th March, 1928. Again, Dr. Drabble played a major part in its establishment, contributing £5,000 of the total building costs of approximately £11,500. The Ministry of Health awarded £2,000, to be paid in annual instalments. In addition, Mrs. Drabble paid about £300 to have the adjacent Nurses' Home (formerly Sans Souci) redecorated for the occupation of the Matron, Miss J. Mather (formerly of Guy's Hospital), and two qualified nurses and two staff nurses who were to assist her. They also had the benefit of a large garden and tennis lawn. Rodney House provided a six-bed public ward, three private wards and a "separation ward", with subscribers from Walton, Hersham and Oatlands taking precedence over those from the surrounding area. For a stay of usually 14 days, a patient in a private ward would pay £7-7s per week, but those unable to afford the £3-3s per week for a bed in the public ward could apply for assistance from their local Maternity and Child Welfare Clinic. In its first two years the home handled 239 confinements with no maternal deaths.

MIDWAY c.1910
This view of the recently-constructed Midway shows some of the nine new houses which had been built there by 1912. The road itself looks less attractive, and the practice of dressing children in large, sturdy boots is understandable when one considers the typical state of the streets at this time. One local resident recalled that "The roads were muddy in winter and dusty in summer.....Sidney Road was almost impassable, full of potholes and mud...", while another remembers how Cottimore Lane, "when we were on the milk round delivering, had to be taken very slowly in case the horse fell as a result of stepping into one of the potholes." Sir Dudley Pound, later Admiral of the Fleet, lived in Midway with his wife at about this time.

HERSHAM ROAD c.1920
This photograph, taken from the junction with Stompond Lane and King's Road, shows the northern end of Hersham Road, with the late 19th century shops at the south end of the High Street in the distance. This is part of a long, straight stretch of road from the High Street to the Halfway which was laid out following the Walton Enclosure Act of 1800 and lies across part of the former Walton Common. It was originally known as Felcott Lane, after a field on the north-east side marked on the Enclosure Map as Felcot Field. The name probably derives from a cottage in a field or open space. On the right of the photograph, behind the tree on the corner of King's Road, is the house used as Walton's first Council Offices from 1902 until the Council's acquisition of Elm Grove in 1921. Note the noticeboard and flagpole by the hedge in front.

WALTON ATHLETIC CLUB 1945

In 1908 Joseph Sassoon offered Walton Urban District Council ten acres of land in Stompond Lane at £500 per acre, together with a contribution of £500 towards the cost of laying it out as a recreation ground. This offer was rejected, but in 1933, despite some local opposition, the Council purchased the land for £7,000 and created the Stompond Lane Sports Ground. The first cinder track in Surrey was laid here in 1939, financed by the King George V Playing Fields Fund. It was here, on 3rd July, 1942, that five enthusiastic athletes met in a thunderstorm to found the Walton Athletic Club, which had grown to over 200 members by 1954 and produced 12 British international athletes in its first 20 years. At one time, more world records were held at Stompond Lane than at any other British track. The photograph shows the first Club Championship, held at Stompond Lane in July 1945. Seated behind the table are (left to right): G.H. Frowde, Chairman of Walton & Weybridge U.D.C.; Jack Hirchfield, one of the five founder members; E.J. Allsop, President of the Club; and Walter Stokes and J.F. (Peter) Harding, both founder members. Another of the original five stalwarts, Jim Rosewell, is sitting on the ground immediately to the right of the table.

WALTON HOSPITAL FETE 1932
Walton Hospital at this time was still supported by public subscription, and the annual hospital fete gave a valuable boost to its funds. Among the stalls on 27th May, 1932, were Mrs. Poupart's holiday stall, Hersham Women's Institute, a refreshment stall run by Mr. J.E. Butt of The Crown Hotel, and a flower and pottery stall in charge of Mrs. Drabble, whose late husband had been one of the hospital's founders and the first Chairman of the Hospital Committee. Mrs. Drabble had also lent the field in Stompond Lane in which the fete was held. In addition, the crowds could enjoy the novelty of film tests at the "Capitol Studio", under the direction of Clifford Spain, and snaps by Nettlefold Productions' cameramen. The 100 ft. Pathe de Bier cameras can be clearly seen in the photograph. The fete was opened by Major Sir Archibald Boyd-Carpenter, M.P. for the Chertsey Division.

A.J. HIRONS' CARTS, CRUTCHFIELD LANE, c.1906
Arthur Hirons (1878-1976) ran a contracting business from Fishmore Farm, off Cottimore Lane, for many years, growing much of the fodder for his horses on the farm. He and his brother, W.T. Hirons, who worked for George Miskin from 1895 onwards, both had houses in Crutchfield Lane, where this photograph was taken. Mr. and Mrs. Hirons are standing on the right. Much of Mr. Hirons' contracting work was for the Walton Urban District Council - for example, in March 1908 the Council accepted his tender of 8s. (40p) per day for removing the road sweepings from the Walton streets to the dump. Hours were long, and Mrs. Hirons was often up at 4 a.m. to help feed the horses and get them ready for the 6.30 a.m. start. When the Walton and Weybridge Councils amalgamated in 1933, Mr. Hirons gave up the contracting business and opened a riding school at Fishmore Farm.

KING'S ROAD c.1910
This view, looking east from the Hersham Road end of King's Road, has changed little since the photograph was taken over 80 years ago. The street was originally named Crutchfield Road, but this led to confusion with the adjacent Crutchfield Lane, and the name was therefore changed c.1900. In November 1908, a resident here wrote to the "Surrey Herald" complaining of the Council's failure to improve the street lighting in King's Road, which had only three lamps for nearly 100 houses. In the right foreground is "Hazeldene", home of Frederick George Stonebanks, Clerk to the Burial Board. In 1911 he opened Stonebanks' Shipping Agency in Bridge Street, which specialised in arranging passages for emigrants to Canada and Australia, and some to South Africa.

ST. ANDREW'S PRESBYTERIAN CHURCH c.1935
From 16th June, 1928, a small band of Presbyterians held a weekly service in the Playhouse, and in July 1930 they purchased this site on the corner of The Chestnuts. The architect P.G. Overall prepared plans for a church to seat 350 and a hall to seat 250. Initially, the hall alone would be built and serve as a church. The Rev. Hugh Macluskie was appointed as acting Minister in March 1931. W.H. Gaze & Sons of Bridge Street commenced building work in September and the foundation stone was laid by Lord Beaverbrook in November. The hall, costing £5,000, was provided with a vestry, parlour, kitchen, cloakroom, lavatories, chair store and transformer chamber. The walls were wainscotted in Douglas fir with red bricks above. The ceilings were covered with "Insulwood" - a patent acoustic board made in Sunbury. "Unity" electric tubular heating (still something of a novelty) was installed by Messrs. Sedgley & Edgley of High Street. Messrs. Gaze's Works Band played at the opening ceremony on Saturday, 20th February, 1932. The intended church building was never constructed, but the "hall" is still in use by the United Reformed Church.

WALTON-ON-THAMES FIRE BRIGADE c.1921

In 1921 a Dennis Brothers motor tender arrived at Walton, reducing response times and providing the firemen with a good supply of water and another ladder. It is shown outside Elm Grove, home of the Brigade from 1921 until the opening of the new Walton Fire Station in March 1969. J.A. Turner, son of the High Street garage proprietor and a fireman since at least 1905, drove the new fire engine. The men were still volunteers and were summoned when needed by a siren on the roof of Elm Grove and by bells in their homes. Behind the new engine is its predecessor, the Shand Mason 300-gallon "Double Vertical" variable expansion steam engine, bought by the Council at a cost of about £345 and delivered in November 1906. When in use, it was originally pulled by two horses. From 1921, however, the new motor tender would have towed the engine. The Chief Officer of the Walton Brigade was Ralph Wilds, the local Council Surveyor, who had succeeded Walter Brind in 1905.

WINCHESTER ROAD c.1914

In 1870 the only turning on the east side of the High Street was Church Walk, but by 1896 Ashley Terrace (later widened to form the southern half of Churchfield Road) and part of Winchester Road had been laid out. The first houses built in the future Winchester Road were the row of ten on the left, known as Winchester Villas. In July 1901, Mr. J. Longhurst and a group of friends founded a Baptist church in Walton, with 11 members who met in a room at 5 The Broadway, in the High Street. In 1902 they acquired a plot of land in Winchester Road and building work by John Lee of Hersham commenced in August 1904 on a chapel to seat 160 people. On November 3rd, 1904, foundation stones were laid by Alderman William Hart, J.P., of Kingston and Mr. J.C. Wollacott of New Malden. This was followed by tea in the Wesleyan Schoolroom and a meeting. The chapel, on the right of the photograph, was officially opened on Monday, 16th January, 1905. It included a "school chapel", and a vestry, kitchen and offices were added soon after. The red and white brick building had cemented interior walls and a matchboard dado, and was heated and lit by gas. One of its earliest Pastors, from September 1909, was Mr. Longhurst's brother, Rev. Caleb M. Longhurst.

ROMAN CATHOLIC CHURCH c.1920

St. Erconwald's Roman Catholic Church in Esher Avenue was opened by Father du Plerny, Rector of St. Raphael's, Surbiton, on Wednesday, 26th May, 1906. The building, considered to be "in keeping with the rest of the houses on this pretty Estate", was designed by G.B. Carvill. The following Sunday, 30th May, Mass was celebrated in Walton for the first time since the Reformation. By 1930, the congregation felt the need for a larger church. On 17th July, 1931, the "Surrey Herald" reported that on the previous Saturday Father O'Beirne's garden fête, held in the grounds of "Oakfields" by permission of Mrs. Mordaunt Christopher, had raised a "princely" sum for the new Walton Catholic Church Building Fund. The new church was erected beside the original building and was officially opened on 16th July 1937. The original church, shown here, is now used as a church hall.

CLAUDIUS ASH & SONS' FACTORY c.1914

In the late 1880s Edward Power, having outgrown the shed behind his father's chemist's shop at 9 High Street, moved to a workshop in Church Walk and by 1896 had built the dental instrument factory shown here. In 1902 he set up a limited company, The Power Manufacturing Company Limited, which was taken over by Claudius Ash, Sons & Company (1905) Ltd. in 1907, with Edward Power as Managing Director. This in turn merged with De-Trey of Kentish Town in 1924 to form The Amalgamated Dental Co. Ltd. They built a large factory complex on the north side of Churchfield Road and the old premises seen here were demolished in 1936, the year in which Edward Power died aged 81.

THE MACHINE SHOP 1967

The Amalgamated Dental Company continued the tradition of excellence fostered by the original parent company and continued to expand the range of products manufactured at Walton and its chemical factory at Addlestone. Many innovations in dental technology were developed here - for example, the firm were amongst the first to adopt chromium plating, and later developed fibre optics in dentistry. Eventually the Walton works provided over 200,000 feet of floor space and employed over 1,000 people. In 1968 the company's name changed to A.D. Engineering Co. Ltd. and continued to manufacture its renowned products for both the home and export market. Photographed in the machine shop in 1967 can be seen components for dental chairs and units in the course of production. Reorganisation of the parent company and the prevailing economic conditions eventually led to the closure of the Walton works on 27th November, 1981.

POLISHING SHOP c.1914

By the outbreak of the First World War the factory referred to locally as Powers Works employed around 100 people. The Claudius Ash company's origins were as London silversmiths in the early 19th century. They made dental fittings in precious metals and became the premier manufacturer of these and associated surgical instruments and requisites for the dental profession with a worldwide market. The Walton factory contained a number of specialised departments which produced a wide range of very high-quality dental tools and equipment. One of the original specialities of Power's company had been forceps and by 1929 the Walton factory was able to produce over 110 patterns of this item alone. Also manufactured here were dental burrs, which by 1966 were being produced at a rate of 9,000 a day. The photograph illustrates part of the early polishing shop with its overhead shafting and leather belting to the individual polishing spindles. On the bench in the left foreground can be seen some more of the products for which the factory was renowned - dental probes and "Ash's Root Elevators".

ARMISTICE DAY PARTY, 1919

In addition to the official celebrations mentioned elsewhere in this book, the end of the First World War was marked by street parties such as this one for the residents of Florence Road, held in a meadow in front of Sassoon's Cottages belonging to Fishmore Farm, now the site of Cottimore Crescent. The party continued with children's games and sports, with prizes for the winners. Seen here are, behind the tables: Mr. & Mrs. Starkey, Mrs. Cole, Mr. & Mrs. Weedon, Mrs. Peck, Mr. & Mrs. Vincent, Mrs. Cox, Mr. & Mrs. White, Mrs. Baker, Mr. & Mrs. Mullett, Mrs. Lock, Sid Coveney, Ernest Mullett, Les. Mullett, Wally Edwards, Doris Cole, Fred Weedon, Molly Johnson, Beat Vincent, the Huckins girls, the Hirons girls, the Peck girls, the Baker girls and Jack Yeates(?).
In front of the tables, from left to right, are Arthur Groves, Bob Cox, John Cole, Alf Cole, Charles Weedon holding Ken Lock, Bob Weedon, Cyril Vincent, Joyce Weedon, Phil Weedon, Ron Cole and Cyril Weedon.

V.E. PARTY, FLORENCE ROAD, MAY 1945

In Walton as elsewhere the end of the war in Europe was marked in May 1945 by spontaneously organised street parties. The celebrations in Florence Road were typical of many, with tables set up in the street outside no. 47 for the children, and residents providing whatever they could from their rations, including such "luxuries" as Spam, cheese sandwiches and jelly. In Cromwell Road ice creams were provided by Mr. Wheatley and oranges were available for the children, while the children of Russell Road were each given an envelope containing money by Mrs. Latter. It was common for these parties to continue with games, dancing in the street and other celebrations. In Russell Road the entertainment included a jazz band, while Cottimore Lane had afternoon sports, pony rides and a ventriloquist.

WALTON METHODIST CHURCH c.1925

In 1886 the Methodists reluctantly sold their chapel in what is now Manor Road to the Walton & Weybridge Gas Company, who wished to enlarge their gasworks. The Methodists received £700 for the property, of which £350 was used to buy a new site at the Walton end of Molesey Road (now Terrace Road). They then set to work to raise the estimated £3,000 required for the building of a new church to seat 450 people and a Sunday School for 170 children. The church was built by Knight's of Chertsey and was opened and dedicated on Thursday, March 15th, 1887. The generosity and initiative of the Church members was such that within 18 months of the opening they had succeeded in paying off all the debts on the building. The red brick church with its 80 ft. spire remains a prominent landmark in Terrace Road and a popular centre for local worship.

GRIDLEY MISKIN'S TIMBER YARD c.1955

In 1885 George Miskin (1865-1937), son of a farmer in Terrace Road, began a small timber yard as a sideline, partly to supply the needs of the farm. The business quickly grew and developed, adding imported woods to its English timber stocks and then branching out into joinery and mouldings. A liaison with Gridley & Co. of Kingston developed during the First World War, and in 1921 the two firms amalgamated to become Gridley Miskin & Co. Ltd., with W.G. Watson and George Miskin as governing directors. The photograph shows George Fry, who joined the firm in 1927 and made local deliveries by horse and cart until the cart was finally replaced by a lorry c.1962. The horse was stabled on the premises in Terrace Road. The firm's 1907 steam engine also remained in use until the 1960s. In 1986 Gridley Miskin was taken over by Sabah Timber Ltd., who were in turn taken over by Harcros, the present owners of the yard, in 1988.

TERRACE ROAD c.1912

At the beginning of this century, Terrace Road and Hurst Road were still a small lane known as Hampton Court Lane. In the words of a local lady, "Civilisation ceased with Miskin's". In 1896 there were only a handful of houses on the south side of the road, but by 1912 Annett Road, Dudley Road, Russell Road, Sunbury Lane and Cambridge Road were all being developed and, as can be seen, housing development was fairly well advanced both there and along the north side of Terrace Road, while the south side remained much as before. The sign in the left foreground offers for sale or to let the large house known as Bishops Hill. The house seems to have been named after Thomas Bishop, a prosperous tanner who lived here in the latter half of the 17th century. It stood just off Manor Road, to the north-west of the Methodist Church, but had a long drive opening on Terrace Road north-east of the church, as seen here. The building subsequently became the home of the Walton Conservative Club.

THE "TIN SCHOOL" c.1923

In 1908, in an attempt to ease the long-standing overcrowding in the village schools, a temporary school for infants and mixed juniors was provided by the Surrey County Council in Terrace Road. The East Walton School opened on 31st August 1908. Another room was added in 1912, by which time the Infants' School in the High Street was so overcrowded that children from Russell Road and further east were refused admission. By August 1914 both the Boys' and Girls' Schools were so full that no children were moved up from the Infants, further aggravating the congestion here. In 1924 the Headmistress, Miss Gardiner, left to become Headmistress of Walton Junior School and was succeeded briefly by Miss S.S. Hanger, and in 1925 by Miss N.L. Brown. At this time the school had 103 children on its roll. It amalgamated with Walton Infants' School when the latter moved to its new building in what is now Ambleside Avenue in 1931, but re-opened in 1933 with four teachers and 139 children. The school is now the Grovelands County First School.

HURST ROAD PUMPING STATION, 1910 & 1975

The pumping station at Hurst Road was opened in 1911 to pump water from the Thames into local reservoirs, principally the Knight and Bessborough reservoirs on the south side of Hurst Road. The photograph above, taken from the embankment of the Knight reservoir, shows the buildings nearing completion. The railway lines shown were for use in the construction. McAlpine and Co. used a 3'0" gauge railway here for their reservoir work from 1908 to 1911. The pumping station has since become a true waterworks, undertaking all the processes of abstraction, storage, filtration, chemical treatment and pumping. By c.1973 it was pumping an average of 120 million gallons of untreated water into the storage reservoirs, and 30 million gallons of treated water into the Dittons and South London water supply. Three bombs fell in the vicinity of the works on 23rd/24th February, 1944, one exploding in a filtration bed within 20 yards of the building and another damaging a reservoir on the other side and fracturing one of the 48" mains carrying part of London's water supply. The waterworks were remodelled in 1964 and again in the mid/late 1970s, when the last two steam engines were finally phased out. The earlier of these was the no. 4 steam unit, one of the four original engines installed in 1911. This was of the tri-compound three-crank marine type, working at a pressure of 200 lb. p.s.i. and running at 120 r.p.m. The 10½ft. diameter flywheel weighed 13 tons. The other steam engine was a 1926 inverted vertical triple expansion type with reciprocating pump, made by Hathorn Davey & Co. Ltd. of Leeds. The interior view below, taken by Howard Lansdell, shows the boiler house, situated in the left side of the building as shown.

THE CAMPS c.1909

Members of the Thames Camping and Boating Association relax on their camping ground opposite the Weir Hotel. The campers would come to Walton each year, often only for weekends, but sometimes for longer holidays, many of them storing their boats at Rosewell's Boathouse during the winter. The newly-arrived campers would order whatever they needed for their stay from one of the local grocers on Saturday, taking away what they required overnight. The shop's delivery boys had to be at work before 7 a.m. on Sunday morning so that they could hire a boat in which to deliver the remainder of the orders before breakfast. Many members also employed local boys to run errands on Saturdays, such as shopping or fetching drinking water from the boathouse. These jobs were very popular, as the campers would pay for the hire of the necessary boats for these errands, giving the boys free boating in addition to what was paid for their labour.

THE CAMPS, 1st MAY, 1908

Flooding had always been a hazard on the low ground in the Thames Valley, and the fertility of some of the meadowland bordering the river actually depended until recent times on the annual spring flood. The construction of the Desborough Cut in 1930-35 helped to reduce the frequency and severity of floods such as that which is illustrated at the camp site on Friday, 1st May, 1908. The following day, the "Surrey Advertiser" reported that "The melting of the heavy fall of snow, followed by continuous rain, caused the river to rise on Monday and Tuesday no less than three feet...Another rise of several inches occurred on Thursday, when the water was only 14 inches below the level of the big flood of 1894."